Cows

by Peter Brady

Bridgestone Books
an Imprint of Capstone Press

Bridgestone Books are published by Capstone Press
818 North Willow Street, Mankato, Minnesota 56001
Copyright © 1996 by Capstone Press
Printed in the United States of America

Library of Congress Cataloging-in-Publication Data
Brady, Peter. 1944–
    Cows/Peter Brady
    p. cm.
    Includes bibliographical references and index.
    Summary: A brief introduction to dairy cows and their life on the farm.
    ISBN 1-56065-344-2
    1. Dairy cattle--Juvenile literature. 2. Cows--Juvenile literature [1. Dairy Cattle. 2. Cows.]
I. Title.
SF208.B735 1996
636.2'142--dc20

                                        95-49903
                                          CIP
                                           AC

Photo credit
All photos by William Muñoz. William is a freelance photographer. He has a B.A. from the University of Montana. He has taken photographs for many children's books. William and his wife live on a farm near St. Ignatius, Montana, where they raise cattle and horses.

Table of Contents

Words in **boldface** type in the text are defined in the Words to Know section in the back of this book.

What Is a Cow?

A cow is a farm animal. Cows are female cattle. Male cattle are called bulls. Dairy cattle are raised for milk. Beef cattle are raised for meat.

What Cows Look Like

Cows have large, heavy bodies and a long tail. They have an **udder** that holds milk. Cows can be black, white, red, brown, or spotted. Cows can weigh from 1,000 to 3,000 pounds (450 to 1,350 kilograms).

Where Cows Live

Cows live mostly in herds. There are no bulls with them. In the summer, cows roam **pastures** eating grass. In the winter, they stay in barns.

What Cows Eat

Cows eat grass, hay, clover, and corn. Cows have no top front teeth and four stomachs. Cows drink over 20 gallons (76 liters) of water every day.

Chewing Cud

Cows swallow their food more than once. They chew until the food is soft enough to go down. Then they spit the food up and chew it again. This is called chewing their **cud**.

Different Kinds of Cows

There are more than 250 **breeds** of cows. Some of them are Holstein, Jersey, Guernsey, and Brown Swiss. The black-and-white Holsteins are the most well known.

Milking

Farmers milk cows twice a day. Some families still milk cows by hand, but most cows are milked by machine. One cow can give up to six gallons (23 liters) of milk a day. That is about 100 glasses of milk.

Calves

Cows have one calf a year. They are pregnant for nine months and give birth in early spring. Calves can become mothers in about two years.

What Cows Give Us

Cows give us milk. Dairy products such as butter, cheese, yogurt, and ice cream are made from milk. Hamburger, steak, and roast beef come from cows. Most of the leather for jackets, belts, and other products comes from cow skin.

Hands On: Make Your Own Butter

You will need one cup (.24 liter) whipping cream and a small glass jar with a screw-on lid.

Pour the room-temperature whipping cream into the jar. Screw the lid on and shake well.

In about 10 minutes, clumps of yellow fat will start to form. Keep shaking until there is a large lump of butter.

Empty the jar into a bowl, and pour off the liquid. This is buttermilk. Rinse the butter with water until there is no more buttermilk.

Press the butter against the side of the bowl with a wooden spoon. Add a little salt to the butter and stir. Now it is ready to taste.

Words to Know

breed—group of animals that come from the same ancestors

cud—food brought up from one stomach to be slowly chewed again

pasture—a field with grass and plants for cows to eat

udder—bag under a cow that holds milk

Read More

Aliki. *Milk From Cow to Carton*. New York: Harper Collins, 1992.

Fowler, Allan. *Thanks to Cows*. Chicago: Children's Press, 1992.

Gibbons, Gail. *The Milk Makers*. New York: Macmillan,1985.

Henderson, Kathy. *Dairy Cows*. Chicago: Children's Press, 1988.

Index